Year of the
Goat

For Norman and Caryl N.S

For Sophie W.A.

Year of the Goat

WAYNE ANDERSON & NIGEL SUCKLING

BARNES
&NOBLE
BOOKS
NEW YORK

This edition published for Barnes & Noble, Inc.,
by arrangement with Pavilion Books

2002 Barnes & Noble Books

M10987654321

ISBN 0-7607-3813-0

First published in Great Britain in 2002 by
PAVILION BOOKS
A member of Chrysalis Books plc

64 Brewery Road, London, N7 9NT

Set in Minion & Ribbon

Printed and bound by Imago, Singapore

Editor's Note

HE WHO UNDERSTANDS OTHERS IS CLEVER, HE WHO UNDERSTANDS HIMSELF IS WISE

HE WHO OVERCOMES OTHERS IS POWERFUL, HE WHO OVERCOMES HIMSELF IS STRONG

LAO TZI: TAO TE CHING CH 33

Long ago, when the Queen Mother of the West still cultivated the Peach Trees of Immortality in her palace atop the Kunlun Mountains of Tibet, and the Jade Emperor still ruled heaven from under the Pole Star, the goat was revered in China as a peaceful and prosperous animal, associated with pastoral and domestic bliss. Ever present in people's lives, its importance and distinctive characteristics led it to be chosen as one of the twelve symbols of the Chinese zodiac.

What follows is an enlightening collection of Chinese legend and lore relating to the astrological sign of the Goat. Against this mythical background, the symbol of the Goat is related to a person's time and date of birth, thereby providing a full and comprehensive personal profile.

Chinese astrology is wonderfully simple to grasp once you have an active picture in your mind of its twelve basic symbols. They are not the random assortment of beasts they might first seem, but were carefully chosen by the ancients to illuminate a complete spectrum of human types. This comprehensive guide will give even those with no previous knowledge of the subject a clear picture of what Chinese astrology has to say about them. Readers will benefit too from useful advice on how they are likely to relate to people of other signs, gaining an understanding, for example, about how clashing year signs need not end in disaster, but, with the right knowledge, be turned into productive and healthy relationships.

Wherever possible sources have been named in the text and can be found in modern translations of the Chinese classics. The folktales are harder to attribute because slightly different versions have gone into each telling, but most still circulate today in traditional areas of China as oral folklore. The spelling used is mostly modern Pin Yin apart from a few already familiar names like Genghis Khan and Confucius.

Tapestries from the Mongolian borders of China sometimes show people riding on the backs of goats like this, while from the opposite pole of the country, far away on the coast of the South China Sea, come tales of gods riding down to earth on the backs of celestial rams.

Introduction
Determining Your Birth Sign

DETERMINING YOUR OVERALL BIRTH SIGN IN CHINESE ASTROLOGY IS AS SIMPLE AS KNOWING THE YEAR OF YOUR BIRTH. THE ONLY COMPLICATION IS THAT THE CHINESE NEW YEAR VARIES, LIKE EASTER, FROM YEAR TO YEAR, BEING SIGNALLED BY THE SECOND NEW MOON AFTER THE SHORTEST DAY OF THE YEAR. SO IT CAN FALL ANY TIME BETWEEN THE LAST WEEKS OF JANUARY & FEBRUARY. OTHER FACTORS SUCH AS THE MONTH, DAY & HOUR PLAY THEIR PART, BUT THE CHINESE BELIEVE THAT IN ASTROLOGY THE YEAR OF YOUR BIRTH AFFECTS YOU MORE THAN ANYTHING ELSE.

For a full list of years and signs see the table at the end of this chapter, but the Goat is your sign if you were born between the dates below.

1 FEBRUARY 1919 – 19 FEBRUARY 1920

17 FEBRUARY 1931 – 6 FEBRUARY 1932

5 FEBRUARY 1943 – 25 JANUARY 1944

24 JANUARY 1955 – 12 FEBRUARY 1956

9 FEBRUARY 1967 – 30 JANUARY 1968

28 JANUARY 1979 – 16 FEBRUARY 1980

15 FEBRUARY 1991 – 4 FEBRUARY 1992

1 FEBRUARY 2003 – 22 JANUARY 2004

The first thing to realize about this sign is that in Chinese the same word is applied to both goats and sheep. Sometimes, goats are called 'mountain-sheep' to distinguish them, just as we might distinguish between a hill-pony and a tame one, but the basic name is the same. In Tibet and neighbouring regions 'mountain-sheep' can also mean the Ibex, a creature that, along with the ox, is considered one of the most holy of them all. Often, the name of this astrological sign is simply translated as 'sheep' but that does not give us the full picture. We have to take the full spectrum of its meanings into account.

To the newcomer, it might seem strange that in Chinese astrology everyone born in a particular year shares the same sign, because there would appear to be no scope for individuality. However, it is not quite as simplistic as it seems. The individuality comes through by taking into account your month, day and hour signs; it's just that the Chinese believe the year has more influence than anything else. And it's not hard to see some truth in this – even outside astrology. In any discussion among people of different generations there is a natural tendency for sides to form according to age. People's views are affected enormously by the climate of the times in which they grew up. Each generation has a perspective shaped by its own experience and set of standards – shaped also by its reaction to and against the generations either side of it. Chinese astrology just takes this further by saying that each year will affect those born within it in a particular way, an effect that can be explained by the character of that year, and that character is defined by a particular symbol.

The year sign in Chinese astrology is said to be a person's Yang or 'outgoing aspect'. It governs the way they behave and interact with others throughout their life. Their Yin aspect, or 'inner person' is designated by their month sign. This is directly equivalent to the month signs of Western astrology and is where individuality begins to enter the Chinese picture.

Luckily, the symbols used for the months are exactly the same as those for the years. This may seem confusing at first, having, say a Goat for your year sign and an Ox for the month. But the beauty of the system is not having to grasp a different set of symbols for each level. You will see how to relate the year and month signs later but for now, just bear in mind the distinction we've made – your year sign is your outgoing or sociable aspect – your month sign represents your private, family self.

Many Westerners prefer to take their month sign as their true Chinese horoscope sign, and they are perfectly entitled to do so, there is nothing in Chinese astrology to forbid it – and possibly it better suits the more individualistic temper of the West – but the Chinese might say you are missing the main picture.

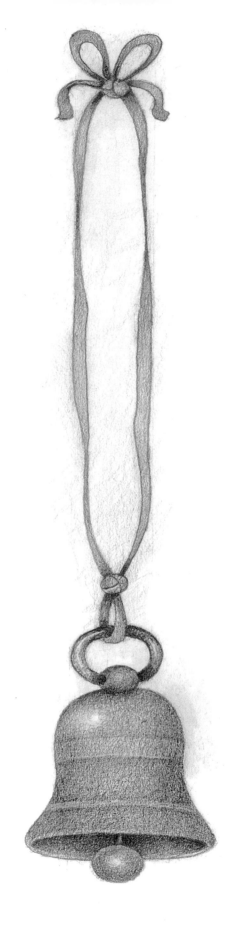

MONTH SIGN

RAT – SAGITTARIUS

OX – CAPRICORN

TIGER – AQUARIUS

HARE – PISCES

DRAGON – ARIES

SNAKE – TAURUS

HORSE – GEMINI

GOAT – CANCER

MONKEY – LEO

ROOSTER – VIRGO

DOG – LIBRA

BOAR – SCORPIO

Most people can find their Chinese month sign by looking at the equivalents above. However, if your birthday falls near the limits of your Western star sign you need a simple calculation to be sure. This is because Chinese months are fixed by phases of the moon, while the sun decides the Western calendar. The correspondence varies from year to year depending on the Chinese New Year.

To check your month sign, look up the date of the Chinese New Year preceding your birthday in the table on page 15. The Chinese months begin pretty much on the same date of each

Through most of its long history, China has taken astrology very seriously indeed. From the highest government levels to the lowliest peasant marriage, people consulted the stars before taking any major decision or starting any new venture. Families would have to be convinced of a couple's compatibility, as shown by their birth signs, before giving their blessings to a betrothal. At heart it was a belief that, to a degree, we are controlled like puppets by unseen powers — which astrology and other forms of divination aim to expose. In modern China, this is officially discouraged and people take astrology probably no more or less seriously than in the West, but old habits die hard.

following month of the Western calendar; beginning with the month of the Tiger and ending with the month of the Ox, which varies in length depending on the start of the next New Year.

This is not perfectly accurate but it works for most people and the thing to bear in mind is that, just like in Western astrology, people born on the cusp between one sign and another will embody aspects of both. The cut-off is not as sharp as people like to think. However, if you want to be sure, check the date of the new moon in your birth month, because every Chinese month begins with the new moon.

For example: in 1979 the Chinese New Year fell on 28 January. Consequently, the month of the Tiger ran from 28 January to 28 February, the Hare until 28 March, the Dragon until 28 April, the Snake until 28 May, and so on. If you were born on 16 March that year, your month sign would be the Hare. As 1979 was a Year of the Goat, in Chinese astrology you are a Hare-Goat. In personal relationships you behave as a Hare while to the wider world you are a Goat. These signs happen to be very compatible so the chances are that you will be someone who is very comfortable with the times in which you live, though not as comfortable as someone who has the Goat as both their year and their month sign.

The day of your birth also has a character but the calculations are too impractical to go into here, considering the relatively small impact it has on your profile. The hour of birth, however, is significant and very easy to assign if you happen to know your time of birth.

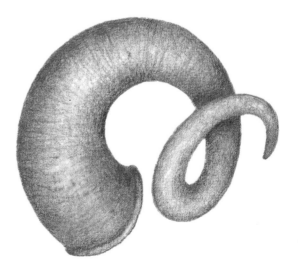

HOUR SIGN

The two factors we have so far, the year and month signs, are enough to tell a great deal about a person, but the sign associated with the hour of birth can be the key to understanding a character. Often called the 'Secret' or 'Hidden' sign, it reveals how we feel in our innermost selves, which is often very different to the face we put on even for our friends and family.

The Chinese day, like the year, is divided into twelve periods. These are governed by the astrological signs, with each two-hour period having a Yang and a Yin half. If you know your time of birth, check the table below to see what your hour sign it is.

	YANG	YIN
RAT	11PM – 12	12 – 1AM
OX	1AM – 2AM	2AM – 3AM
TIGER	3AM – 4AM	4AM – 5AM
HARE	5AM – 6AM	6AM – 7AM
DRAGON	7AM – 8AM	8AM – 9AM
SNAKE	9AM – 10AM	10AM – 11AM
HORSE	11AM – 12	12 – 1PM
GOAT	1PM – 2PM	2PM – 3PM
MONKEY	3PM – 4PM	4PM – 5PM
ROOSTER	5PM – 6PM	6PM – 7PM
DOG	7PM – 8PM	8PM – 9PM
BOAR	9PM – 10PM	10PM – 11PM

Taking once again the example of 16 March 1979: if you were born at 2.30pm this would mean that your inner sign is a Yin Goat, perfectly matching your year. But if you were born the night before at 1.30am, your hour sign would be the Ox, which could create tension as the Ox and the Goat clash.

Rat	Ox	Tiger	Hare	Dragon	Snake	Horse	Goat	Monkey	Rooster	Dog	Boar

			Year: 1927	1928	1929	1930	1931	1932	1933	1934	1935
		Chinese New Year begins on:	2 Feb	23 Jan	10 Feb	30 Jan	17 Feb	6 Feb	26 Jan	14 Feb	4 Feb
		Element associated with that year:	Fire	Earth	Earth	Metal	Metal	Water	Water	Wood	Wood

Rat	Ox	Tiger	Hare	Dragon	Snake	Horse	Goat	Monkey	Rooster	Dog	Boar
1936	1937	1938	1939	1940	1941	1942	1943	1944	1945	1946	1947
24 Jan	11 Feb	31 Jan	19 Feb	8 Feb	27 Jan	15 Feb	5 Feb	25 Jan	13 Feb	2 Feb	22 Jan
Fire	Fire	Earth	Earth	Metal	Metal	Water	Water	Wood	Wood	Fire	Fire
1948	1949	1950	1951	1952	1953	1954	1955	1956	1957	1958	1959
8 Feb	29 Jan	17 Feb	6 Feb	27 Jan	14 Feb	3 Feb	24 Jan	12 Feb	31 Jan	18 Feb	8 Feb
Earth	Earth	Metal	Metal	Water	Water	Wood	Wood	Fire	Fire	Earth	Earth
1960	1961	1962	1963	1964	1965	1966	1967	1968	1969	1970	1971
28 Jan	15 Feb	5 Feb	25 Jan	13 Feb	2 Feb	21 Jan	9 Feb	30 Jan	17 Feb	6 Feb	27 Jan
Metal	Metal	Water	Water	Wood	Wood	Fire	Fire	Earth	Earth	Metal	Metal
1972	1973	1974	1975	1976	1977	1978	1979	1980	1981	1982	1983
16 Feb	3 Feb	23 Jan	11 Feb	31 Jan	18 Feb	7 Feb	28 Jan	16 Feb	5 Feb	25 Jan	13 Feb
Water	Water	Wood	Wood	Fire	Fire	Earth	Earth	Metal	Metal	Water	Water
1984	1985	1986	1987	1988	1989	1990	1991	1992	1993	1994	1995
2 Feb	20 Feb	9 Feb	29 Jan	17 Feb	6 Feb	27 Jan	15 Feb	4 Feb	23 Jan	10 Feb	31 Jan
Wood	Wood	Fire	Fire	Earth	Earth	Metal	Metal	Water	Water	Wood	Wood
1996	1997	1998	1999	2000	2001	2002	2003	2004	2005	2006	2007
19 Feb	8 Feb	28 Jan	16 Feb	5 Feb	24 Jan	12 Feb	1 Feb	22 Jan	9 Feb	29 Jan	18 Feb
Fire	Fire	Earth	Earth	Metal	Metal	Water	Water	Wood	Wood	Fire	Fire
2008	2009	2010	2011	2022	2013	2014					
7 Feb	26 Jan	14 Feb	3 Feb	23 Jan	10 Feb	31 Jan					
Earth	Earth	Metal	Metal	Water	Water	Wood					

YOU NOW HAVE A PROFILE OF YOURSELF IN CHINESE ASTROLOGICAL TERMS. WHAT THIS ALL MEANS SHOULD BECOME CLEAR LATER, BUT FIRST LET'S TAKE A LOOK AT WHAT CHINESE HISTORY, MYTHOLOGY AND FOLKLORE HAVE TO SAY ABOUT THE GOAT BECAUSE THESE HAVE ALL HELPED SHAPE THE SYMBOL OF THE GOAT USED IN ASTROLOGY.

The Chinese calendar is the longest unbroken chronological record in the world, having been devised in 2637 BC by the first legendary Chinese emperor, Huang Di, in the sixtieth year of his life (or possibly of his reign – records from that time are hazy).

Huang Di and the other early emperors are semi-mythical beings said to have been part dragon and to have had divine powers. Probably, like King Arthur, their stories began with real historical figures and grew somewhat in the telling. Besides the calendar, Huang Di is also credited with the discovery of the wheel and the compass, for having written the first treatise on medicine and for being the father of the Chinese people.

Huang Di invented the sixty-year cycle by which all major events in Chinese history have been dated ever since. The figure of sixty was arrived at by combining the twelve annual signs of the zodiac with the five elements of philosophy. These correspond (though with different names) to the four elements of Western philosophy plus the fifth element or 'quintessence' that unites all the rest.
In China, the four elements are Metal, Water, Wood and Fire, and the fifth, or quintessence, is Earth.

The zodiac signs are also sometimes called the 'Twelve Earthly Branches', because they are the channels through which the divine manifests itself in the world. The five elements, in their Yin and Yang aspects, are likewise often known as the 'Ten Heavenly Stems'.

Chapter one

The Goat in Legend and Lore

ART, AS IT WERE, IS NATURE; JUST AS NATURE, SO TO SPEAK, IS ART.

THE HAIRLESS HIDE OF A TIGER OR LEOPARD IS ABOUT THE SAME AS THAT OF A DOG OR GOAT.

ANALECTS OF CONFUCIUS 12:8

Sheep and goats, along with dogs, pigs, cattle and poultry, were among the earliest domestic animals in China, and part of the everyday scenery for the mostly rural population. This common aspect of the animal is vital in grasping the meaning of the astrological sign. As with most of the other creatures of the Chinese zodiac, it is a totem beast chosen partly because people could immediately relate to it without need of explanation.

On this everyday level, the goat and sheep mean much the same in China as in the West. They are associated with pastoral peace and plenty because flocks thrived during those times.

Domestic sheep are considered docile and easily led, rams assertive and strong – while goats, well, everyone knows what goats are like. The big difference, though, is that Christianity adopted sheep and lambs as major symbols at the heart of its teachings, while in China it is just one of several important symbols that are all overshadowed by the dragon.

This is why, in Chinese astrology, it can be helpful to think of this sign as the Goat or the Ram rather than the Sheep. The docile nature of the common sheep is definitely an aspect of the sign, but the traits of the ram and the goat are equally present.

Emperor Shun was the last of the five legendary emperors who preceded the first historical Xia dynasty, which lasted from about 2000 – 1500 BC. Before Shun, legend says there were ten suns which took turns to light each day, but when Shun took the throne they all rose up into the sky together in protest. They would have scorched all life from the earth had Shun not ordered his great archer Yi to shoot nine of them out of the sky. Since then we have had just the one sun. This trauma was followed a while later by floods that threatened to drown the world. Shun set his minister Yu to control them, and he was so successful that Yu became emperor himself, founding the first Xia dynasty, because he was the first emperor to be succeeded by his own son.

The Dragon is the only purely fabulous beast in the Chinese zodiac, the rest are all everyday creatures. Or, in the cases of the Tiger and the Snake, hopefully not everyday creatures, but in the distant past there was certainly the possibility that they could intrude on people's lives at any time. All of the creatures do, however, have supernatural associations – myths and legends describing their role in the primeval shaping of the world. The supernatural creature immediately suggested by the Goat in China is the *xiezhi*, the legendary unicorn-goat that possessed a divine instinct for justice.

Eighty miles or so north-west of Peking is a palatial cemetery where the emperors and empresses of the Ming dynasty are interred, along with their favoured courtiers. From a great arch

ANCIENT WOODEN CARVING OF A CHARGING XIEZHI FROM GANSU PROVINCE IN NORTHERN CHINA, WEST OF PEKING.

A UNICORN-GOAT OR *XIEZHI* STATUE FROM THE SACRED WAY WHICH LEADS TO THE MING TOMBS NEAR PEKING. THE CREATURE'S BACKWARD-SLOPING HORN IS ALMOST HIDDEN IN THE FUR ON ITS HEAD. THE STATUE DOES LOOK DISTINCTLY STURDIER THAN MOST GOATS, IT'S TRUE, BUT NOTE THE CLOVEN HOOVES.

which is one of the architectural wonders of the world, the wide avenue called the 'Sacred Way' or 'Spirit Walk' leads to the main tomb complex. It is lined with larger than life-sized statues of real and legendary beasts, each portrayed in squatting and standing poses. In order they are: lions, unicorn-goats, camels, elephants, true unicorns or *Qi lin* and horses.

The *xiezhi* is a legendary creature said to have the talent of distinguishing between the innocent and the guilty. The most famous one dates from around the third millennium BC, the era of Emperor Shun. Besides much else, Shun is famous for introducing the first codes of law and subsequently bringing civil order and justice to China. They were implemented by his Justice Minister Gao Yao, but even Gao Yao in all his wisdom could not always decide the truth of a case. When this happened he would call for his infallible, divine she-goat to be brought into court. Commanding her to butt the accused, their fate would be decided by whether or not she did.

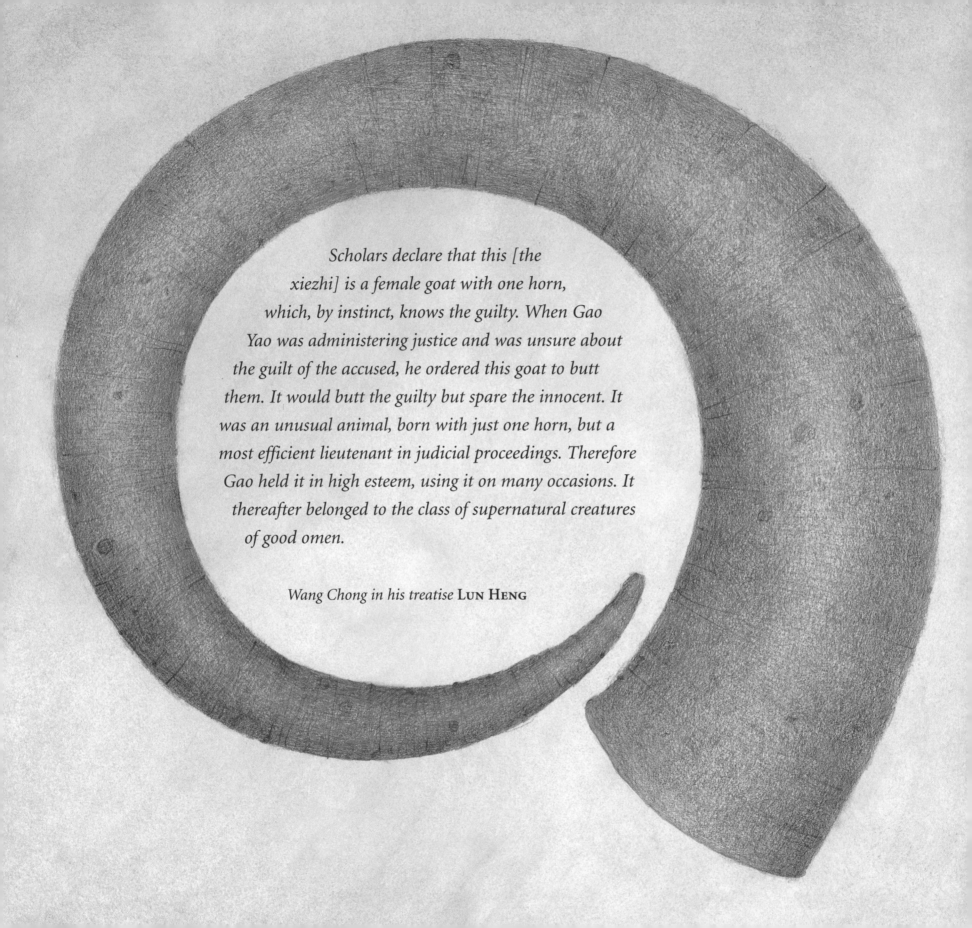

Scholars declare that this [the xiezhi] is a female goat with one horn, which, by instinct, knows the guilty. When Gao Yao was administering justice and was unsure about the guilt of the accused, he ordered this goat to butt them. It would butt the guilty but spare the innocent. It was an unusual animal, born with just one horn, but a most efficient lieutenant in judicial proceedings. Therefore Gao held it in high esteem, using it on many occasions. It thereafter belonged to the class of supernatural creatures of good omen.

Wang Chong in his treatise LUN HENG

This creature became revered along with the likes of the dragon and the phoenix as a divine beast of good omen; and for much of history Chinese magistrates had its image embroidered on their hats or robes, or painted on the walls of their chambers as a sign of integrity. Often guarding the entrance would be two large statues or silk hangings showing a male and female *xiezhi*. Not only were these to intimidate plaintiffs trying to cheat justice, but they were also supposed to keep an eye on the officials themselves. Corrupt officials have always been bane of the common people in China and there are countless folktales that relish them meeting their comeuppance. So it was long believed that any magistrate bold enough to wear or display the sign of the *xiezhi* must be at peace with the creature and therefore trustworthy, and many officials took care to encourage this belief.

Emperor Shun's gifted *xiezhi* is the most famous of all but it was not the first or last. Emperor Huang Di, Shun's legendary predecessor, is said to have been presented with a *xiezhi*. 'What does it eat and where does it live?' the emperor asked. 'It eats *jian*,' came the reply, referring to an unknown type of plant. 'In summer it lives in marshy areas. In winter it lives where evergreens and cypresses grow.'

There are other tales in many parts of China of one-horned goats with similar powers that once belonged to local rulers or officials. Pictograms from the Shang dynasty (c. 1500 – 1000 BC) on oracle bones often show the *xiezhi* with a single horn with two side prongs. In Chinese calligraphy, this became part of the compound character for justice along with the sign for water, which is also a symbol of justice because it always seeks the level.

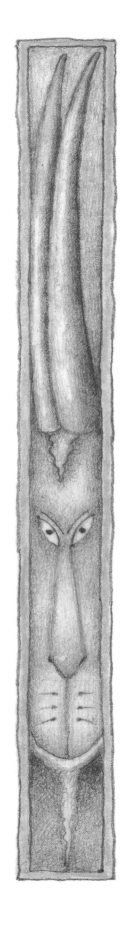

Other records from the Shang mention in passing that grass favoured by the creature is particularly good for rush matting, but there is possibly confusion here between the *xiezhi* and some other natural creature, maybe the *ibex*.

The *xiezhi* may seem to be a completely fabulous creature but it is perhaps worth mentioning that in Ethiopia during the Middle Ages they seem to have developed a technique for producing one-horned deer, goats and cattle. They did this by fusing their horn buds soon after birth so that they took root in the skull together, sprouting as a single horn. These creatures were then given as diplomatic gifts to monarchs ranging from India to Europe, increasing the mystique of Ethiopia as the home of unicorns, Prester John and the Queen of Sheba.

Unicorn-goats and sheep are also supposed to occur naturally, though very rarely, from time to time. Certainly in China, there is a firm tradition of it happening occasionally. Also, that such creatures seem to have been blessed with some of their famous ancestors' divine gift for sensing the truth.

A UYGUR FOLK TALE

Because of the goat's link with the legendary xiezhi, goatherds

and shepherds are often depicted in folklore

as delivering justice for the common people

through the possession of some magical talent or instrument.

Such stories are particularly popular because of their heroes'

humble status in the everyday world.

Once, long ago,

there was an orphan named Aniz

who became a shepherd for his village landlord.

He was happy enough in his humble work

and popular because he was always friendly

and could play the flute like an angel.

Whenever people heard him playing they would stop whatever

they were doing to listen, their eyes misting over with sweet

dreams and memories.

Aniz's greedy employer, who took a percentage of most villagers' earnings, noticed this idleness and grew furious at the thought of what it was costing him. So, one day, on some trumped up charge, he sacked Aniz, had him soundly thrashed and broke his flute into tiny pieces.

Aniz ran away weeping both for himself and his instrument, which had been his last reminder of his parents. He meant to run away into the wilderness, but on the way bumped straight into an old man and fell in a sobbing huddle at his feet.
'Come, come, my boy,' said the old man kindly, patting his shoulder. 'Nothing can be as bad as all that. Why don't you come and tell me all about it over a cup of tea?'

At the old man's house, Aniz told his story over fragrant cups of the most delicious tea that had ever passed his lips. There were also cakes sweeter than he had ever imagined, so that soon the world began to seem not such a terrible place after all. As he listened, the old man took a bamboo and carefully fashioned a flute, which he finally handed to the boy. Its song was so sweet and true that Aniz immediately fell in love with it and began to play even better than before.

'How would you like to work for me?' the old man asked. 'I have flocks that need tending and, what is more, I have a plan for teaching that old landlord a little lesson.' Then he explained his idea to the boy.

For a while, life went on much as before, only now Aniz tended someone else's sheep and took care not to play his flute when people were around, so the landlord had no further cause to hate him. His audience became the creatures of the wild woods where he sheltered his flock at night. At dusk, they all gathered round his campfire under the spell of the music. Many were usually enemies, but as long as the flute played they forgot this. The fox settled down by the rabbit, the tiger with the goat. And none of the hunters ever touched Aniz's sheep at other times. Rather they guarded them as fiercely as they guarded Aniz himself.

Then one night, the wicked landlord dreamed of a beautiful white hare with a mark on its head like a crescent moon. The hare was pounding leaves with a pestle and mortar and the landlord immediately knew it was the magic hare that lives on the moon and makes an elixir of eternal youth from the leaves of the sacred cassia tree there.

'That's right,' the magic hare said to him in the dream. 'And see this marking on my head? Find a hare with that mark and you too can start your life anew.'

The landlord woke in great excitement because death was the thing he feared most – even more than losing all his money. Calling his three sons, he promised half his wealth to whichever of them found the hare of his dream. Only, to be fair, he let the eldest son go looking first because he stood to lose half his natural inheritance.

The eldest son wandered aimlessly along, worrying about losing out to a brother. Then he bumped into an old man. 'You look like you have a burden on your mind, my son,' the old man said. 'Why not share it with me?' The youth explained his problem but the old man only laughed: 'Why, you've nothing to be afraid of. If such a hare is to be found, my shepherd Aniz will know because he is the friend of all wild creatures. And if it is not to be found, well, your inheritance is safe anyway.'

Much relieved, the eldest son hurried off to find Aniz, who agreed to help if the son returned that evening with a hundred pennies. When the eldest son returned, Aniz settled down to play his flute as usual. Soon the wild beasts began emerging from the shadows of the trees and among them was a white hare with a crescent marking on its head, just as the landlord had seen in his dream. Aniz handed it to the eldest son saying: 'Keep a tight hold, because it's none of my business if it escapes.'

The young man hurried home but had not gone far when Aniz's flute trilled out again. The hare struggled, broke free and ran off into the night. The son searched everywhere and then went back to Aniz for help. But the shepherd only shrugged and said; 'I told you to hold it tight.' So the youth had no choice but go home and tell his sorry tale.

The other two sons then tried their luck with Aniz, but each time it turned out the same. Their father was so angry that he decided to try for himself. Laden with strings of cash he found Aniz and asked him to play his flute as before. Aniz took the money and raised the flute to his lips – but this time the only creatures to emerge from the shadows of the trees were the hunters – the wolves and bears, tigers and leopards and they closed around the landlord with a hungry light in their eyes. Terrified, he threw himself at Aniz's feet and begged: 'Please! Spare my life and I'll give half my worldly goods to the poor!'

The landlord was as good as his word and Aniz became a local hero, with flocks of his own and a ready audience for his flute whenever he chose to play. The greedy landlord never again tried acting against him, and became a much nicer person altogether for the rest of his long life. So perhaps his dream did come true, though not quite in the way he had imagined.

Due to their association with peace, prosperity and good times in general, goats and sheep were traditionally a favourite animal for sacrifice to the gods and ancestors, just as they are in the Bible. In fact, in ancient China, the ancestors were often paid far more attention than the gods because they could be trusted to listen more closely to the supplicant's concerns. Just because someone had died did not mean they left the family. It simply meant they were now in the spiritual realm and could speak the language of heaven, so they could represent the family's interests to the gods far more directly than those left behind on earth. The family head that died became more important than ever and was considered a very real guest at all major social occasions.

As the keepers of sacrificial sheep and goats, shepherds were sometimes credited with prophetic powers, like the one in the poem below:

Your shepherd comes, bringing kindling and wood

With the wild cockerel and hen for sacrifice

Your rams come, sturdy and unblemished

None limp and none sicken

He waves them on into the (sacrificial) stall

Your shepherd dreams of locusts and fish

He dreams of pennants and flags waving

A sage interprets the dream, saying:

'Locusts and fish mean years of plenty

Flags and banners mean many guests and celebrations.'

Song from the *Shi Jing*, one of the Five Classics upon which all traditional Chinese scholarship was based from before the age of Confucius until modern times.

THE FIVE RAMS OF CANTON

Goats and sheep are also strongly linked with the discovery of rice, China's staple food since the dawn of time, particularly in the city of Guangzhou, formerly known as Canton. Guangzhou is the capital of Guangdong Province on the southern Chinese coast. It is one of the greatest city ports of China and is also often called the City of the Five Rams.

This comes from a legend that long ago five immortals robed in the five mystical colours flew down on the backs of heavenly rams at that spot on the coast. Each carried a seedling of rice that they gave to the starving humans there, promising that if they took care of them they would never know hunger again. And so it has proved because to this day the temperate climate of Guangdong ensures that its paddy-fields produce up to three crops a year, plus an abundance of other fruits and vegetables which are exported to less favoured regions.

The Ram is an appropriate emblem for the Cantonese people because, if one is permitted such broad generalizations, their character reflects the astrological sign in all its aspects.

In their exemplary cultivation of both agriculture and the arts they reflect the peace-loving, civilizing influence of the domestic sheep. In their sturdy independence from the rest of China they reflect the ram, the bold leader of the flock. This independence of spirit shows in the strong dialect of the region that can be impenetrable to outsiders. It also shows in the unfavourable comparisons you often hear in everyday talk there between Canton and distant Beijing, in the cold north, where flowers die in winter and the spring festival has to be celebrated with artificial blooms. In Canton, they proudly point out, flowers blossom the whole year round and the extravagant Cantonese Spring Flower Festival is famous throughout the East.

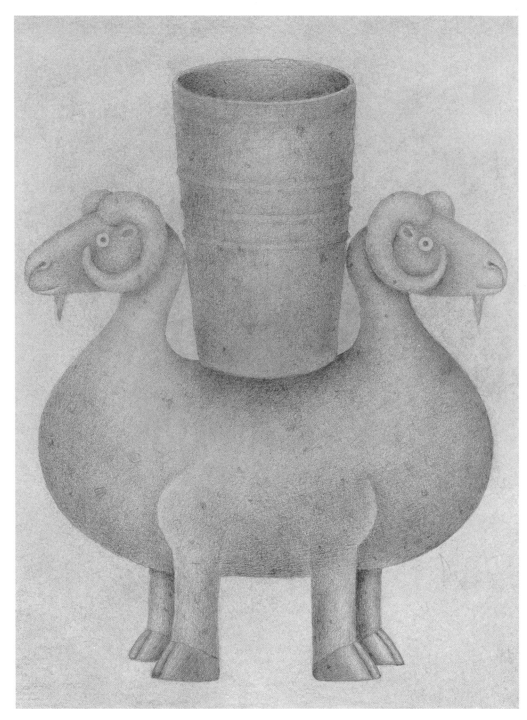

Ceremonial cauldrons like this ritual wine vessel from the Shang dynasty are among the finest early Chinese bronze castings. The bronze cauldron or *ding* had the same importance as altars in other cultures.

Finally, the Cantonese also reflect the adventurous mountain goat because since ancient times their trading ships have fanned right out across the South China Sea and as far afield as India, Arabia and Africa. A great number of them have also settled abroad, often only returning after generations when they have made their fortunes. These descendants generally receive as warm a welcome from their relations as if they had grown up together, though there is inevitably a degree of rivalry over which party did best by either staying or leaving.

The five Canton immortals are not the only celestials known to ride on goats' backs. A very popular god, one of the Gods of the Eight Directions named Huang Chu Ping, is also famous for it.

In his youth Huang Chu Ping was a goatherd. One day, when he was about fifteen years of age, he wandered far from home and just kept on going.

Finally, he came to some mountains and a lonely cave where he settled into the life of a hermit. For forty years he meditated. He had, meanwhile, a brother who became a priest and had never given up hope of finding Huang Chu Ping, even after all the time that had passed. This brother happened to pass nearby the cave and called to visit the famous hermit that he had heard about. To the astonishment of them both, he recognised his long-lost brother. After they had caught up on each other's news he finally asked: 'But what became of your herd, brother?'

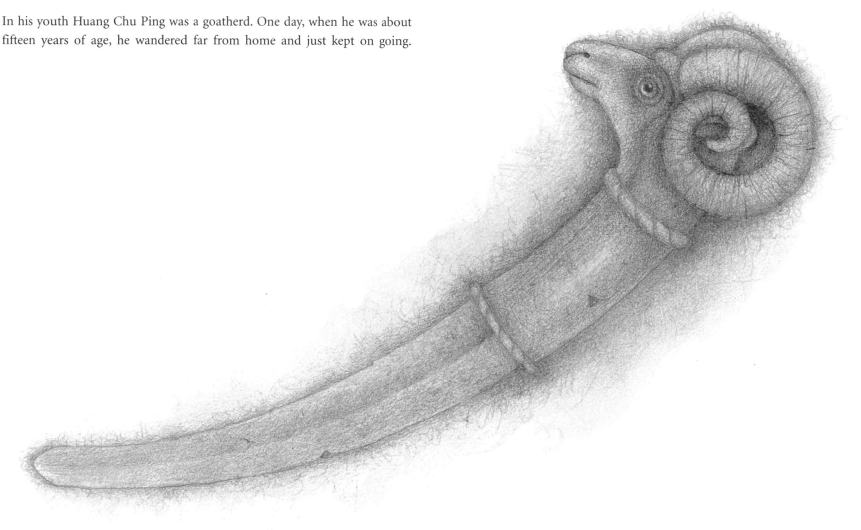

Huang Chu Ping looked puzzled for a while, then brightened and replied: 'But I still have them all here with me!' With that, he touched one of the many large stones lying nearby and they all came to life as goats. 'See,' he said, 'I have taken good care of them all this time.'

Huang Chu Ping went on to become a very famous and popular saint, particularly around Hong Kong where one finds shrines and temples in his honour to this day, and he is often depicted riding on the back of a goat. In Japan, he is known as Koshohei.

THE EIGHTH GODDESS

So in China the goat is associated with justice, fertility and other blessings of civilization; but in practice, being a goatherd is a very humble occupation. Few rich fathers would want their daughters falling in love with one, and this disdain prevailed also in heaven, judging by the story of the Eighth Goddess.

It is commonly said in China that there are seven sacred flowers – azalea, chrysanthemum, lily, lotus, peony, red rose and white rose – each of which has its goddess. But what has almost been forgotten is that there was once also an eighth sacred flower and goddess, the narcissus, whose deity was Bayan Har. She was the youngest and most beautiful of the goddesses and she might have grown even more beloved in China than Kuan Yin the Compassionate had she been able to resist the promptings of her heart. One year, during the eight goddesses' annual trip to earth, they met a goatherd in the Qinling Mountains and Bayan Har fell passionately in love with him. She knew that love for a mortal was forbidden but on her return to heaven she could not put him out of her mind. So finally she slipped away and returned to earth to marry her beloved.

TOMB STATUE OF A CHIMERA WITH RAM'S HORNS AND WINGS.

The dowager Empress of Heaven, Xi Wang Mu, the formidable Queen Mother of the West, was furious when she learned about this. She despatched her troops to fetch back the wayward goddess and banished her to the lonely frozen mountains far to the west of China that have since taken her name. Here, the goddess turned to stone but her tears continued to flow, turning to streams and rivers and finally the great Yellow River itself which was named from the colour of her favourite flower, and of her tears.

In this way, Bayan Har managed to reach out to her lover, for the river ran straight to his country. But when Xi Wang Mu heard of this she raised a chain of mountains in the path of the river, forcing it to wander far away north into Mongolia before it could find its way back. Thus even this small contact between Bayan Har and her goatherd in the Qinling Mountains was denied them, but in astrology the narcissus has ever since been the lucky flower of the Goat sign.

Finally, goats and sheep are famous in China as symbols of filial piety because when young they kneel as if praying to suckle from their mothers. Statues of rams are often placed in the 'spirit path' of officials' tombs as filial piety is so highly prized among such officials.

Chapter two

The Astrological Sign of the Goat

MAN AT HIS BIRTH RECEIVES HIS FATE AND BY IT EACH LIFE MUST BE DISPOSED

Qu Yuan FROM HIS POEM *EMBRACING THE SANDS* C. 280 BC

In Chinese astrology, the sign of the Goat has absorbed all the associations mentioned in the last chapter, on top of all the natural ideas a rural people would have about a creature that lived alongside them in their daily lives.

Two or three thousand years ago, when the Chinese zodiac was devised, there were probably many other influences that we can only surmise about. All that is certain is that when it came to choosing twelve totem animals to represent the full spectrum of personality, the Goat was included. That is how important it was in people's lives at the time. Legend tells us that the creatures were chosen by either God – the Jade Emperor

– or the Buddha, depending on who is telling the tale. He declared a race and named the months after the animals as they arrived. The Rat came first by cunningly riding on the Ox's back and jumping off at the last moment to scamper across the winning line. (The Rat also tricked the Cat into missing the race, which is why cats have hated rats ever since.) The Goat, meanwhile, ambled in comfortably in eighth place behind the Horse and just ahead of the Monkey, making no great enemies along the way. That is one of the characteristics of the Goat. People with the Goat for their sign can be stubborn and assertive but mostly they are friendly and sociable and willing to accommodate others.

GENERAL CHARACTER TRAITS OF THE GOAT

All that this great Earth contains, within the Six Harmonies and between the Four Seas, is illuminated by the Sun and the Moon, and traversed by stars great and small. It is all ruled by the four seasons and embodied in the grand annual cycle. All creatures that are born from the deities and the spirits have their different forms. Some are short-lived, some are long-lived. Only the Wise One can fathom the Way of the Universe.
Classic of Mountains and Seas Prologue Chapter 6

What follows is an outline of the Goat personality in Chinese astrological terms, but you must remember that unless your year, month and hour signs all happen to be the Goat, you cannot expect to match the profile very closely. Most people are a mixture of often conflicting signs by birth, and how they manage the interaction is what establishes their individuality. This is just the template or archetype of the Goat.

The goat and the sheep in China are associated with peace and prosperity because real goats and sheep thrive during such times. Hence it is also linked with the other refinements of civilization that prosper during times of peace, such as the arts, philosophy and religion. People born under the sign of the Goat are generally said to be charming, diplomatic, imaginative, loving, libidinous, generous, sociable, artistic, adaptable, loyal and lucky. They can be stubborn and aggressive when threatened, but Goats rarely go out of their way for a fight.

In its aspect of the domestic sheep, the sign most typifies the enjoyment of peaceful times, but it must be remembered that Westerners need to compensate for their own slant on this animal. The sheep does typify peacefulness in China but not to the same extent as in the West where it is a byword for people who will follow any leader rather than make up their own minds. The aspects of the goat and the ram are strongly present in this sign.

Passivity and being easily led, however, are indeed among the negative aspects of the Goat sign. Qu Yuan said in his poem *Embracing the Sands* (c. 280 BC): *To censure greatness and doubt the unusual, such is the nature of the herd.* But this is only one of several negative tendencies of the Goat. Every sign has these;

QU YUAN (332-296 BC) IS ONE OF CHINA'S GREATEST AND BEST-LOVED POETS. HIS DEATH IS COMMEMORATED EVERY YEAR BY THE DRAGON-BOAT RACES HELD ON THE FIFTH DAY OF THE FIFTH MONTH. THE STORY GOES THAT ON THAT DAY, HAVING BEEN BANISHED IN DISGRACE FROM HIS NATIVE KINGDOM OF CHU, HE THREW HIMSELF INTO THE MILUO RIVER IN HUNAN PROVINCE AND DROWNED. THE RACES RECALL FISHERMEN'S EFFORTS TO SAVE HIM, BUT THE FESTIVAL ALSO MARKS THE DAY WHEN DRAGONS WERE SUPPOSED TO LEAVE THEIR UNDERWATER PALACES FOR THE SKY IN ORDER TO MAKE THE SUMMER'S RAIN. THE FESTIVAL'S DUAL PURPOSE IS TO REMIND THEM OF THIS AND AVERT DROUGHT.

they are the reverse of its virtues. The Horse, for instance, has a bold, venturesome character but in negative mode tends towards reckless and selfish adventure. So, passivity is one of the Goat's negative traits, but to a much lesser extent than people tend to imagine in the West. More characteristic of the Chinese Goat is impatience with petty discipline and regulations.

The Goat and the Horse signs, incidentally, are very complementary and people with these characters tend to get along famously despite their different approaches to life. The Goat appreciates the Horse's warlike tendencies because they help guard its peace, while the Horse respects that gratitude –

plus the civilized comforts the Goat has to offer after the battle is won, not to mention sexual favours. A Year of the Horse tends to be wild and adventurous, while the Year of the Goat that follows tends to be more tranquil and ordered.

Being naturally unassertive, sociable and lacking in ego makes the Goat an easy friend and partner, but Goats can be surprisingly stubborn if pushed too far. Dominating people often try to take advantage of their good nature and are then surprised when their docile friend suddenly says 'no,' and means it.

On the negative side, Goat people are generally considered poor at managing their finances, though more often through generosity than recklessness. This needs to be tempered either by other elements in their birth chart or by seeking out more level-headed partners. Another negative trait is over-sensitivity. Empathy with other people's feelings is one of the Goat's shining virtues, but it can be taken too far. Pessimism, self-pity and low self-esteem are also to be found in the Goat gone sour, along with evasiveness and cowardice. But all these vices are rare because Goats are usually blessed with luck and have little cause to become embittered.

The Goat is a romantic, sensual sign and in marriage and other partnerships is most naturally compatible with the Boar and the Hare; also, through the attraction of opposites, the Horse and the Tiger. The Goat gets on well with most signs in fact, though rarely the Ox. This may seem surprising since the Ox is also a great lover of peace and the arts of civilization; but the Ox tends to be more serious, disciplined and frugal than the Goat and so they rub each other up the wrong way. The Rat and the Dog also have difficulty with the Goat.

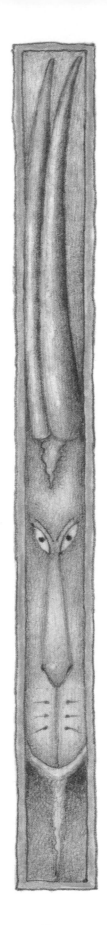

A FARMHOUSE ON THE WEI RIVER

In the slant of the sun on the countryside
Cattle and sheep trail home along the lane
A rugged old man by a thatched door
Leans on a staff and thinks of his son, the herd-boy.
There are whirring pheasants, full wheat-ears
Silk-worms asleep on pared mulberry-leaves.
The farmers, returning with hoes on their shoulders,
Hail one another familiarly.
No wonder I long for the simple life
And am sighing the old song, Oh, To Go Back Again!

WANG WEI

ELEMENTS

Although the signs recur every twelve years, they are influenced each time by a different one of the five elements – Metal, Water, Wood, Fire and Earth. These give the sign a slightly different character each time so it is in fact sixty years before any one returns in exactly the same form. This sixty-year span is known as the 'Great Cycle' or *Tai Sui* and is the basis of all Chinese chronology. See the chart on page 15 for the element affecting your birth year.

In addition to this cyclic element, every sign has a fixed one as shown in the chart opposite. The Boar, the Rat and the Ox are associated with the element Water and the North. The Tiger, the Hare and the Dragon are associated with Wood and the East. The Snake, the Horse and the Goat have Fire and the South; while the Monkey, the Rooster and the Dog have Metal and the West. In this context, the element Earth is not usually directly linked with any of the signs because it represents the centre. Years when the sign's natural element coincides with the rotating one of the Great Cycle are considered especially fortunate because all the sign's natural tendencies will be reinforced.

Next we will look at the ways in which each element affects the fundamental character of the Goat.

METAL GOAT

17 February 1931 to 6 February 1932 – 15 February 1991 to 3 February 1992

THE ELEMENT METAL

POSITIVE QUALITIES: *strength, success, perseverance, honesty*

NEGATIVE QUALITIES: *stubbornness, inflexibility*

ASSOCIATED PLANET: *Venus*

Effect on the Goat: Metal boosts the Goat's confidence and self-assurance, though less than it may appear. This Goat remains vulnerable and sensitive below the surface and this can lead to jealousy and possessiveness if not recognised by their loved ones. The element attracts gold, so this Goat will usually be well rewarded in whatever field it chooses, but has to guard against too lavish spending on home luxuries and the arts.

WATER GOAT

5 February 1943 to 24 January 1944 – 1 February 2003 to 21 January 2004

THE ELEMENT WATER

POSITIVE QUALITIES: *creativity, adaptability, empathy, fluency, wit, intuition*

NEGATIVE QUALITIES: *inconsistency, lacking in motivation*

ASSOCIATED PLANET: *Mercury*

Effect on the Goat: Water has quite the opposite influence to Metal on the Goat, bringing out all the friendly, sociable, generous impulses of the sign. Water Goats are generally well-loved by most people around them and often have an air of helplessness that brings out the chivalry in others. But they should guard against being too self-effacing and pliant. This can lead to a feeling of being taken for granted that eventually leads to a most embarrassing backlash. Luckily, the Water Goat attracts loyal and forgiving friends.

WOOD GOAT

24 January 1955 to 11 February 1956

THE ELEMENT WOOD

POSITIVE QUALITIES: *strength, honesty, generosity, flexibility, unselfishness, ability to inspire others*

NEGATIVE QUALITIES: *not recognising own limits*

ASSOCIATED PLANET: *Jupiter*

Effect on the Goat: Wood has the virtue of being strong but more flexible than Metal, so this Goat should fall somewhere between the two previous signs in being naturally quite assertive while remaining diplomatic and accommodating. Cheerful, tactful, generous and trusting, this sign has a tendency to be a bit too trusting sometimes and it is often up to their genuine friends to save them from being taken advantage of. Luckily there are usually plenty of these at hand.

FIRE GOAT

9 February 1967 to 29 January 1968

THE ELEMENT FIRE

POSITIVE QUALITIES: *decisiveness, passion, positivity, inventiveness, courage, determination, perception*

NEGATIVE QUALITIES: *impulsiveness, selfishness, impatience*

ASSOCIATED PLANET: *Mars*

Effect on the Goat: Because Fire is the Goat's natural fixed element, all the more active qualities come to the fore. Fire Goats are generally anything but passive sheep, they are the mountain goat personified. Ambitious, graceful, charming and inventive, Fire Goats make bold artists and art patrons. Being more outspoken than other Goats often makes them less popular but they do not particularly care. Fire Goats are great dreamers and benefit from down-to-earth partners.

EARTH GOAT

28 January 1979 to 15 February 1980

THE ELEMENT EARTH

POSITIVE QUALITIES: *patience, attention to detail, reliability, prudence, sympathy, discipline*

NEGATIVE QUALITIES: *selfishness, lack of imagination*

ASSOCIATED PLANET: *Saturn.*

Effect on the Goat: This Goat is more careful with money than the others, though still far from being a miser by anyone else's standards. Earth gives it the discipline and perseverance to see projects through, but under pressure can lead to over-caution and worry. Optimistic and caring, the Earth Goat readily attracts friends and admirers. It can be quite sensitive to criticism, but tends to hide this.

Chapter three

Friends and Enemies

I HAVE NEVER YET MET A PERSON WHO COULD PERCEIVE HIS OWN
FAULTS & BRING THE CHARGE HOME AGAINST HIMSELF.

ANALECTS OF CONFUCIUS 5:26

You should now be more familiar with your Chinese astrological profile. If your year sign is the Goat, it will be coloured by its particular element in the year chart (page 15). This is the face or character that you present to the world. It will influence your opinions about life in general and throughout your life you will view the world through the prism of your birth year.

You will also have a month and possibly an hour sign to fill out the picture. If they happen to be the Goat, then by rights the last chapter should have painted a very familiar picture indeed. You are likely to be one of those contented souls who are rarely at odds with themselves. However, this is not always a good thing because it can lead to complacency and an irritating (to others) certainty that your own viewpoint is the only possible one.

Most people, however, have other signs for their month and hour that will harmonise or clash to varying degrees. The chart opposite is a guide. The quick rule is that signs linked by a triangle are friends. Signs that are opposite are enemies, and the rest lie somewhere in between.

If your year sign is the Goat and your month or hour sign is the Ox, you can expect to often be torn in your judgement and enjoyment of situations. This is not necessarily any worse than if they were in perfect harmony because the whole basis of Chinese philosophy is that when two opposites are resolved they produce something greater than the sum of its parts. Often enemies are more useful than friends for letting us know the true sum of our worth.

When considering conflicts within your birth chart it is worth bearing in mind what the year, month and hour signs represent. The year sign represents the character you display to the world at large; the month is the character you show in individual relations with other people, while the hour sign represents your innermost feelings about life.

To many people, the hour sign is the most crucial because their private feelings are more important than anything else in their lives. When this is in harmony with their other signs this is fine; but if there is a natural clash, then work needs to be done if the person doesn't wish to go through life as a misfit.

Generally speaking, Chinese astrologers consider the month sign as being next in importance to the year sign, so we'll consider that. For those born in the sign of the Goat, the most harmonious sign – apart from the Goat itself – are the Boar and the Hare, two other peace-loving signs. If your year and month signs are both the Goat, there is the danger of being too sure of yourself and not listening to others, but apart from that it is a happy combination. The Boar and the Hare are possibly better partners because they are your natural allies, but they have different perspectives on life. These three signs share a love of peace and order and the blessings of civilization. They excel in the arts, especially the Goat and the Hare, and are probably the calmest and kindest of the signs.

The sign least compatible with the Goat is the Ox, and the others fall somewhere between the extremes. See the review of signs below for details.

The same procedure can be followed with your hour sign. Mark it on the chart on page 51 and see how well it sits with your month and year. If it is in direct opposition to either, this may explain why your reaction to situations is often not what you expect. Unless your goals and achievements satisfy your innermost self you will never be happy with your lot in life. On the other hand, conflict is not inevitable if enough thought, patience and understanding are applied to the problem.

The chart can also be useful for gauging how well you will relate to other people. When their year signs are in harmony, people tend to find it very easy to get along on the first encounter, but whether they will be able to take the relationship further depends on the other factors in their charts. Even though their year signs may match, if their month and hour signs clash they will soon experience misunderstandings. Traditionally, no family would consider approving a wedding match before having the couple's birth charts examined for trouble. It is worth remembering, however, that signs can clash without it necessarily being about right and wrong.

Faced with an enemy, people fall easily into the trap of assuming they are in some contest between good and evil. Sometimes this may be true, but far more often, both sides are right and wrong to similar degrees. The clash arises from differences in outlook and values. So, for the Goat, the big thing to remember is that when you meet the Ox, whether within your birth chart or in other people governed by the sign, there will immediately be sparks and irritation and conflict. The Ox is your natural enemy in the stars just as you are its natural enemy, but that doesn't mean either of you is intrinsically more in the right. You are born to disagree, but if you can overcome your differences you will make an unbeatable team.

REVIEW OF THE SIGNS

RAT *Shu*

KEYWORDS: AMBITIOUS, PRACTICAL, CHARMING, QUICK-WITTED

The Rat is one of the Chinese signs that Westerners find hard to take to their hearts, along with the Snake and the Boar (or Pig). But to the Chinese all the signs are equally positive – except perhaps for the Dragon, which is held in a far more exalted position and which everyone would like to be able to claim as their own sign.

To understand the Rat in Chinese astrology we must look back two or three thousand years to when the system took shape. In those bucolic days the sight of a rat was often a cause for celebration because everyone knew they were most attracted to the rich peasant's barn. Conversely, rats were famous for abandoning farms where bad luck and a poor harvest were about to strike.

Because of this association with wealth, a Rat's Blessing is still said to attract wealth and happiness. The rural Chinese traditionally encouraged rats into their barns in the hope that they would bring prosperity with them; and when rats were heard scrabbling in the shadows they were said to be counting their money.

In Peking, the third day of the New Year is when people celebrate the Rat's daughter's wedding. The exact date varies around the country but the same ritual is observed in most regions. On that night, householders and their families go to bed early so as not to disturb the rats' nuptials and they leave seeds and other delicacies sprinkled in the corners of their houses and barns for the rats' feast. In return, they hope to be rewarded with a good harvest. In Fujian Province, in the south, legend also says that it was the Rat who gave the first rice seeds to humankind, so we owe it a portion of the harvest in return.

Rats are also famous in Chinese astrology for their intelligence which, as anyone who has kept a pet rat will tell you, is one of the first impressions they make. When not forced to scavenge for their lives in the sewers, rats are charming, sociable creatures; very cat-like in their behaviour in fact, and equally intelligent.

People born under the sign of the Rat are generally optimistic, intelligent, popular, hard-working and dependable. They are imaginative and adaptable to new circumstances. Ambitious, practical, charming and quick-witted, the danger for the Rat is getting carried away with its own cleverness and going too far. Other negative tendencies include being miserly, manipulative and secretive.

The Rat and the Goat do not get along easily. The Rat finds the Goat too woolly-minded, generous and lazy, and the Goat finds the Rat too sharp, clever and bossy for comfort. But as with all natural enemies, if they can solve their differences they make a formidable partnership.

OX *Niu*

KEYWORDS: PATIENT, RELIABLE, DETERMINED, INTELLIGENT, STRONG, PERSEVERING

A popular legend says the Ox was originally a star deity living in heaven. Seeing how hard humans had to work for their food, the Jade Emperor one day sent the Ox star down to teach them agriculture, so that they could expect to eat every third day. But the Ox confused the message, saying they would eat three times a day by following his instructions. As punishment, the Ox was banished from heaven and obliged to keep his rash promise by helping the humans plough their fields. This legend is commemorated by the star many oxen still have on their brows.

The Ox is a symbol of peace because, like the Goat, it flourishes in peacetime. In gratitude for its faithful labour many Chinese will not eat beef, and some Emperors even made this a criminal offence.

People born under the sign of the Ox are dependable, patient and hard working. They will often achieve success later in life when others are abandoning ambition for thoughts of retirement. Their quiet perseverance often succeeds where more volatile characters like the Tiger, the Dragon and the Horse fail. However, this does leave them with such negative traits as lack of imagination, over-seriousness, dullness.

The Ox is the least compatible sign with the Goat, whom it considers flighty and frivolous. They are often thrown together by circumstance, however, and have to rub along as best they can. Like it or not, they are good for each other and equally vital for a happy community. Both are tolerant signs, however, and often their mutual friends will be unaware of the animosity between them.

TIGER *Hu*

**KEYWORDS: PASSIONATE, AMBITIOUS,
BRAVE, CONFIDENT, IMPULSIVE, POWERFUL**

With its strength and courage, the Tiger is the king of the animals. In some areas people dare not even whisper its name, but will refer to it instead as the King of the Mountains or da chong, which means 'large insect'. Traditionally, when a district was troubled by a tiger the people would not try to hunt and kill it, but would leave offerings and politely ask them to move away, which it seems they often did.

The White Tiger represents the west and autumn: as the Black Tortoise does the north and winter, the Green Dragon the east and spring and the Red Phoenix the south and summer. Therefore the Tiger is the patron of the harvest and is often shown carrying the god of the district on its back. It is also the Lord of Death.

People born under the sign of the Tiger are brave, strong and outgoing. They are never happier than when righting some real or imagined wrong and protecting the weak. They like to be the centre of attention and are natural and inspirational leaders, always firing other people up with their ideas. Their negative traits include impulsiveness, a quick temper and recklessness.

The Tiger and the Goat get along famously and make a formidable team in marriage or business; the Tiger making bold forays into the unknown while the Goat ensures there is a happy and welcoming base for it to return to.

HARE *Tu*

KEYWORDS: SOCIABLE, GENEROUS, ARTISTIC, INTUITIVE, MODEST

The Hare (or Rabbit) is one of the friendliest and gentlest of the signs. Though timid by nature, it is also nimble, sensitive, and proverbially clever.

The Hare is also a symbol of long life. It lives with the Goddess of the Moon, Chang O, and spends its time pounding roots of the sacred Cassia (Cinnamon) tree with a pestle and mortar to make an elixir of immortality. At the mid-autumn festival people ask Chang O to sprinkle some of the elixir to grant them longer lives, but people born under the sign of the Hare have less need of this because they tend to be blessed with long lives anyway.

The common hare or rabbit is said to thrive during periods of sound government, and the Empress Wu of the Tang dynasty famously built a Temple to the Hare. Legend says that once, when the Buddha was starving, all the creatures of the forest brought him food. The rabbit had nothing to offer so it leaped onto the fire and gave itself. In gratitude, the Buddha set the rabbit's face on the shining face of the moon where it can be seen today.

People born under the sign of the Hare or Rabbit are mild, generous, graceful, kind and peace-loving. They are adaptable and sensitive, sociable and popular, and tend to be lucky with money. Hares are perfectionists at work and often make good artists and craftsmen. On the negative side, they can be over-sensitive to criticism and surprisingly stubborn at getting their own way.

In Indo-China, the totem animal for this month is not the Hare, but the Cat and despite their very different natures in reality, the characteristics of the two astrological signs are much the same; the Cat being viewed as the graceful house cat that has charmed and beguiled humans since the earliest times.

The Hare and the Goat tend to be the best of friends, sharing a taste for the arts and the more sophisticated refinements of life. Both are modest creatures, so find it easy to blossom in each other's company instead of melting into the audience, as tends to happen around more extrovert characters such as the Dragon.

DRAGON *Long*

KEYWORDS: MAGNIFICENT, INSPIRING, DECISIVE, BOLD, IMAGINATIVE

The magnificent dragon is one of the most popular creatures in Chinese art because it symbolises the Chinese spirit more than anything else. While to the West it is a purely fanciful creature – the only one in the zodiac – the Chinese used to consider it real, pointing to the dragons' bones on sale in every market, which for centuries were excavated from massive deposits found in various parts of China. The earliest emperors were said to be half dragon by blood and to have supernatural powers, particularly over the weather. Later emperors adopted it as their symbol and whenever the dragon is used in this sense it is shown as having five toes, otherwise it only has four.

A Year of the Dragon is lucky for everyone, and a good time to start new ventures, but there is a danger of getting too carried away. Signs that are not as naturally in tune with the Dragon as the Monkey or the Rat are should be especially careful of getting caught up in the mood and attempting the impossible. However, it should otherwise be an exciting and rewarding time all round because all creatures admire the Dragon, even its natural astrological enemy, the Dog. Up to a point anyway. Marriage or partnership between Dragon and Dog tends to be very hard work.

People governed by the sign of the Dragon are generally flamboyant, exciting, ambitious, charismatic, energetic, popular and loud. They are often to be found in a circle of admirers and accept this as natural. Dragons plan things on a grand scale and are unafraid to storm heaven itself to get what they want. They are also great motivators of other people. On the negative side they can be insensitive, inconsiderate and overconfident; and when their plans fall apart they can become very sorry, miserable shadows of their old selves, but this rarely lasts long.

The Dragon and the Goat are not especially close in astrology but from a slight distance they respect each other. The Goat admires the Dragon's boisterous energy and is attracted to its lavish celebrations but usually feels overwhelmed by the Dragon's immediate presence. The Dragon on the other hand appreciates the Goat's concerns but gets impatient with the details.

SNAKE *She*

KEYWORDS: MYSTERIOUS, INTELLIGENT, DISCIPLINED, TASTEFUL

In China, as in other parts of the world, the snake is regarded equally with fascination and dread. Being related to the dragon, it features in many ancient legends and often approaches divine status, but it is also a common and dangerous creature that you could come across at any time. Some snakes are highly prized as culinary delights and their flesh is also said to be good for the eyesight. Many are used in medicine, especially their livers.

The Snake (or Serpent) is a Yin creature closely associated with the female. If a pregnant woman dreams of a black snake it is a sign she will give birth to a girl, while if anyone has a significant dream about a snake it means a big life change is coming. Because it regularly sheds its skin, the snake is a symbol of immortality through rebirth. The Snake is sometimes associated with wiliness and treachery and there is a popular Chinese legend about a demon white serpent that seduces young men to her dinner table (as the main dish) in the form of a voluptuous young woman. But the Snake is better known for repaying kindness and good deeds with treasure, near which it likes to nest. Keeping a snakeskin in the house is believed a sure way of attracting wealth.

In astrology, the Snake is considered wise, clever, mystical, determined and graceful. It is less showy than the Dragon but often more effective for that very reason. Snakes make great diplomats because they can cloak their immediate reactions to situations and appear cool and calm in the midst of crisis, but they will usually make their true feelings known when the time is right. Snakes are very patient that way and therefore make bad enemies. They have long memories and like to leave this life with an even balance sheet. On the negative side, Snakes have a tendency towards manipulation and deviousness that needs to be kept under control. They also have to guard against becoming over-secretive and miserly.

The Snake and the Goat have very complementary characters and can make great partners in love, life and business, though to succeed each needs to be very conscious of its own negative tendencies.

HORSE *Ma*

KEYWORDS: ADVENTUROUS, BRAVE, SOCIABLE, INTELLIGENT

The Horse is a symbol of nobility, strength, courage and war in China. For centuries the only real threat to China came from the nomadic horse riders of Mongolia and the steppes beyond, the same hordes that occasionally ravaged Europe. Known as the *Xiongnu* or simply 'the barbarians', the Chinese built their Great Wall to keep these marauders out and also spent vast sums building up their own cavalry. Horses therefore came to represent the strength and security of China and cavaliers were at least as admired as the knights of mediaeval Europe.

The Horse also has mystical association with the Chinese unicorn or Qi Lin which, along with the Dragon, was one of the first creatures born after the Creation. The unicorn was linked with sages and good emperors for thousands of years and made an appearance when one died or was born. Confucius's birth and death are said to have been heralded this way.

In astrology, the Horse represents nobility, elegance, speed, strength and courage. Horses tend to be optimistic, generous, loyal, honest and practical. They also tend to be forever restless for new horizons; either literally in the sense of travel, or metaphorically in the kind of work they do. They are not the kind to settle happily into a rut as long as it pays the bills. They need constant challenges. Because of this restlessness they can make difficult partners in marriage, but are basically loyal and honest and if given a free rein will repay it by remaining true.

The Horse and the Goat naturally get along very well by dividing life's duties between them. While the Horse is off patrolling the frontiers the Goat is happy to cultivate and improve the territory it is protecting. Emotionally they are well matched, each supplying what the other lacks.

GOAT *Yang*

KEYWORDS: IMAGINATIVE, CHARMING, CULTURED, SENSUAL, ADAPTABLE, LOYAL

See chapter two for a detailed outline of the Goat's temperament, but what we can perhaps emphasize here is that for many Chinese the most important quality the Goat represents is filial piety. Through most of China's long history this has been considered one of the cornerstones of a well-ordered society, and the image of a young goat kneeling respectfully to feed from its mother has a corresponding importance.

This reverence extended beyond the family to elders in general and this respect continues today. Chinese people tend not to celebrate their individual birthdays in a large way. They prefer to celebrate altogether at the New Year, but turning sixty is considered a very important milestone because it means a person has lived through a complete cycle of the years and is better able than others to understand how life works. Old age is considered the pinnacle of life and Confucius himself did not consider himself fully wise until old age. As he says in his Analects: 'At fifteen, I had my mind bent on learning. At thirty, I stood firm. At forty, I had no doubts. At fifty, I knew the decrees of Heaven. At sixty, my ear was an obedient organ for the reception of truth. At seventy, I could [at last] follow what my heart desired, without transgressing what was right.'

MONKEY *Hou*

KEYWORDS: ENTERTAINING, WITTY, CLEVER, IMAGINATIVE, ADAPTABLE

Tales of the Monkey god and his antics are as familiar to Chinese children as *Jack and the Beanstalk* is to ours. The most famous one tells of how the Monkey was once set to guard the Peach Trees of Immortality in the garden of the heavenly Queen Mother of the West, Xi Wang Mu. These peach trees bear fruit only once every three thousand years, and at this time the Queen Mother holds a great feast to share the precious peaches out among the immortals, for it is the peaches that preserve their everlasting life. However, on the eve of one banquet the Monkey ate the lot. As punishment, he was sent to India with various companions (including the Pig) to fetch some original copies of the Buddhist scriptures, because those in China had become corrupted. After many adventures which tested his courage, wit and ingenuity to the limit, the Monkey returned with both the scriptures and great wisdom, and has been revered as a god ever since, though he has not completely lost his taste for mischief and practical jokes.

The Monkey personality is bright, witty, entertaining and popular. The Monkey has a nimble mind and can turn a hand to almost any occupation. Keen to help others with their many talents, they will delight as much in praise as in monetary reward. The downfall of the Monkey is often their irrepressible curiosity and sometimes misplaced sense of fun. They are usually at their best when in the service of others, when loyalty may override the instinct for mischief. Female Monkeys tend to be less troublesome than the males and often in them it is only the virtues of the sign that show.

The Monkey and the Goat tend to get along very easily as friends and casual acquaintances, though in marriage their different approaches to life can cause strains.

MONKEY TEACHES FOX A LESSON

The Monkey is a favourite character in Chinese folklore, famous for its clever wit and sense of mischief. Typical of the stories about it is this one, reputedly told by the Buddha himself:

Once, long ago, all the animals of field and forest grew fed up with the Fox and his sly, stealing ways. They determined to teach him a lesson but none of them could think up a plan until the Monkey had a bright idea. Lying in wait for the Fox one day (but making it seem like an accident) the Monkey casually asked him what he thought was the tastiest food in the world. Well, thinking about food was one of the Fox's favourite games, so he enthusiastically started going through all his favourite delicacies, trying to decide which was the best of all, until the monkey interrupted, saying:

'I've heard that the tastiest food in the world is a bite of the Horse's rump. But hardly anyone has ever tasted it because they do not know the trick.'

'What trick? What trick?' asked the Fox, jumping up and down with excitement.

'Well,' said the Monkey. 'What you must do first is find the Horse lying down asleep; and as it so happens I saw him doing this just a little way back through the trees. Then you must creep up and tie your tail to the Horse's tail, otherwise you won't be able to hold on. You must tie it tightly, but not so tightly as to wake him up. Then you take a big bite of his rump and let me know if it truly is the most delicious food in the world.'

Well, the Fox was delighted by this adventure and followed the Monkey's

instructions to the letter. He crept up on the sleeping Horse, tied his tail tightly to its tail and then took a great big bite of the Horse's plump, juicy haunch.

The Horse lunged to its feet in alarm and plunged kicking and rearing like a dervish around the clearing. The Fox opened his mouth in fright and fell to the ground. The Horse then galloped away like a thunderstorm through the trees, with the Fox bouncing along the ground behind it like a bundle of washing.

When the Monkey saw this he laughed so hard he fell out of his tree and landed with a tremendous thump on his bottom, which is why he has had a red bottom ever since, though it was worth it just to teach the Fox a lesson. The Fox, too, was never quite the same afterwards and has had a speckled coat ever since from scraping along the ground. The Horse, meanwhile, took to sleeping standing up.

'And that Monkey,' Buddha is supposed to have concluded his tale, 'was me in a former life.'

AN IMMORTAL FROM THE HEAVENLY ISLES OF THE EAST

ROOSTER *Ji*
KEYWORDS: FLAMBOYANT, BRAVE, PROTECTIVE, RELIABLE

The Rooster (or Cockerel) is said to possess the five great virtues of literacy, strength, courage, benevolence and loyalty, and in many parts of China roosters are so respected that it is unheard of to eat one outside of famine. Hens, of course, are less fortunate.

The Rooster is considered to be a scholar – partly because his comb looks like an old-fashioned scholars' hat. His strength lies in his spurs and his courage is shown by his willingness to fight to the death over his territory. The Rooster is generous and always calls his wives to share in food when he finds it. He is loyal because he stands guard over his family and never fails to wake the farm at dawn. He is also believed to guard his farm against fire and demons.

In astrology, the Rooster represents all these virtues and is considered well suited to administration and government, or any occupation that calls for both leadership and a careful eye for detail. Roosters have the tendency to be arrogant, overbearing, argumentative, pompous and over-ambitious, but they generally rise above it and are usually forgiven because of their finer qualities. Vanity is also a danger because Roosters are flamboyant in their dress, but again, other people tend to make allowances.

Curiously, female Roosters seem not to be expected just to be 'hens'; that is, passive, not very bright and destined for the pot as soon as they stop laying eggs. Female Roosters share most of the good qualities of the male, but are more modest and usually achieve their ends with much less fuss and need for attention.

The Rooster and the Goat, easy going creature that it is, usually get along very comfortably.

HOW THE DOG BECAME MAN'S BEST FRIEND

In Canton, as we saw in chapter one, legend says that the gift of rice was made to humans by five immortals who rode down to earth on the backs of celestial rams.

In other parts of China, however, they have different accounts and here is a popular one in which the Goat does not shine quite so well.

Long ago, after the Great Flood, goes the legend; the gods and the immortals that lived in the Heavenly Isles of the East took pity on the plight of starving humans. Seeing how they had to scavenge and hunt desperately for food, often themselves becoming the food of tigers and other wild beasts, the Jade Emperor called a great meeting to decide how to improve the people's lot. Finally the Five Grains God stood up and said: 'Why not teach them how to cultivate the rice that grows here in such abundance? Then they will not need to go hunting and expose themselves to all the perils of the jungle.'

DOG *Gou*

KEYWORDS: LOYAL, SOCIABLE, BRAVE, SENSITIVE, INTELLIGENT, OUTGOING

The Dog is man's oldest and most loyal friend in the animal kingdom and in all its varieties, traditionally played a large part in the everyday life of the Chinese; from peasants to ladies at court whose lapdogs lived like royalty.

In astrology, the Dog is considered brave, loyal, intelligent, honest and open. The Dog does not particularly seek money or fame, ranking feeling useful and appreciated more highly, but it is quite able to take a leading role when needed. The Dog is idealistic and a good judge of character. It is generally not easy to fool, but loyalty can blind it to the imperfections of superiors or family members. Dogs tend to be popular, good-looking and attractive to members of the opposite sex. There are exceptions, but less so than with most signs. Most dogs are not naturally aggressive but they are quick to defend what they see as right, and with force if necessary.

Unfortunately, the Dog and the Goat are natural enemies in astrology, tending to see just each other's negative sides. This is curious, because they share many traits, including getting along easily with most other signs, but somehow their differences really grate. The Dog finds the Goat lazy, self-indulgent and slightly devious while the Goat finds the Dog insensitive, bossy and simple-minded; but if they settle their differences they can make a great pair and bring out the best in each other.

This idea set all the other immortals thinking and soon it was agreed to send humans other blessings as well – the Ox and the Horse to pull their ploughs and carts, the Goat to give milk and wool, the Rooster to wake everyone in the morning, the Dog to guard their barns, and the Pig to give meat for the feast in return for its life of idleness and ease.

Soon these creatures were gathered by the shore to cross the great sea to China, but then a problem arose. Which of them was to carry the rice? Thinking of the long and dangerous swim ahead, each of the animals made some excuse or other, except for the Dog. The Dog had been the most moved by the suffering of humans so he volunteered to bear the precious cargo of grain. First he dived into a sticky pool, then he rolled about in a granary until he was covered in rice.

The creatures dived into the choppy waves and began their swim to the mainland, but the Dog lagged far behind the rest. Weighed down by rice, he struggled with the waves until he thought he would surely drown. Finally he crawled onto the shore of China, more dead than alive, with just a few precious grains of rice still clinging to the tail he had mostly kept above the waves. These were enough, though, to plant the first small plot of rice humans had known, and from that came all the rest so that soon it became the staple food of the Chinese. So the Dog became the humans' closest friend in the animal kingdom and to this day many Chinese often reward their dog with a bowl of the best rice at dinner. Cattle and horses meanwhile, have to make do with rice straw, while goats, roosters and pigs get the husks.

BOAR *Zhu*

KEYWORDS: CHEERFUL, SENSUAL, TOLERANT, EASYGOING, GENEROUS

In mythology the Boar (or Pig) is famous for having been one of the Monkey's companions in the great quest for lost Buddhist scriptures, and was rewarded by being made an immortal in the Western Paradise. In everyday life the Pig was one of the earliest domestic animals in China and the character in calligraphy for 'family' is the sign for 'roof' above the one for 'pig'. The pig became a symbol of wealth and contentment because for the peasant it was an insurance against hunger and a great provider for feasts on special occasions. Pork is one of the favourite dishes of the Chinese, especially at New Year because although they are very fond of the pig as an animal, they are just as fond of eating it.

In astrology, people governed by the sign of the Boar are considered honest, reliable, cheerful, sensual and sociable. They generally strive more for domestic bliss than power, but are surprisingly able to take the lead when necessary. Their best qualities show in times of crisis when they bring their full intelligence to bear on the problem. Otherwise, they have a tendency to do only as much as is needed for a good life. The negative traits of the Pig are all those we tend to think of first in the West – laziness, greed and selfishness – but it must be remembered that in astrology these are only as common as the negative traits of any of the other signs.

The Boar and the Goat are naturally the greatest of friends; not quite as close as the Goat and the Hare perhaps, but almost.

Chapter four

Strengths and Weaknesses

UNDERSTAND A PERSON'S FAULTS AND YOU WILL DISCOVER HIS VIRTUES.

ANALECTS OF CONFUCIUS 4:7

Every sign has its strengths and weaknesses and Confucius's saying above expresses a belief that underlies Chinese astrology; that the strengths and weaknesses of a sign are simply two sides of the same coin. Given a congenial life the virtues can be expected to shine, and vice versa. The point is always to remember that every sign is considered equally good overall, with the possible exception of the imperial Dragon. All the signs have their natural enemies, as we saw in the last chapter, but only because their temperaments happen to clash. In the overall scheme of things no sign is intrinsically better or worse than another. Each does best in certain circumstances and badly in others. The trick is knowing when to give free rein to your natural instincts, and when to restrain them until more favourable times come along.

When signs clash it is because they tend only to see each other's faults. Their perception of each other is distorted, which is why it can be a positive thing to have clashing signs in your birth chart. If they can be reconciled, they have between them a very clear grasp of reality because they cover each other's blind spots. Similarly, partners in business or marriage who have clashing signs can make an inspired team if they manage to work through their differences; though in practice it often takes more effort than people are prepared to invest.

So what Confucius and astrology say is that if you clash with someone, you should, in theory at least, be able to divine their hidden virtues from the nature of their vices (or what you perceive as their vices). With the Boar, for instance, gluttony as a vice becomes sensuality as a virtue. The same impulse lies behind both but in gluttony it has got out of control. With the Ox a similar thing applies to stubbornness to the point of stupidity as a vice becoming perseverance and trustworthiness as a virtue. With the Horse it is recklessness and courage. The same impulse can be either a vice or a virtue depending on how it is exercised and balanced with other tendencies.

The idea that one's faults and one's virtues are just two sides of the same coin offers a key to how negative tendencies can be redeemed. Sometimes there is no choice in life but to repress a negative trait with all possible willpower, but unless the impulse behind it is then positively channelled it is wasted. The impulse is merely repressed. In certain cases this may be the only way to deal with a vice, but usually there is a more creative angle.

If, as a Goat, you clearly recognise in yourself all the Goat's negative traits of being indecisive, lazy, over-sensitive to criticism and a doormat for the bolder characters around you, Chinese astrology points a way to turning them around. People all too easily fall into the trap of overcompensation when trying to break bad habits. With being too meek, for example, the temptation may be simply to demand to get your own way all the time. Well, sometimes this works and sometimes it can even be a good thing, but if you're not used to being assertive the chances are that most of the time you will just alienate the people around you and lose valuable friends. Being assertive is not in itself always a good thing, you also need to have good grounds for it.

At their best, people governed by the sign of the Goat are sensitive to other people's feelings and not unnecessarily demanding of attention. So, suddenly becoming callous and self-centred is unlikely to feel any more comfortable to the Goat than being trampled on. What's required is just a bit more assertion at times when it is right – being prepared to dig your heels in and stay firm when it matters. Anything done often enough becomes normal, so by doing this occasionally even the meekest Goat can find their natural balance. The aim is to become a positive Goat, not a Tiger or a Dragon.

Your year sign defines the cultural climate in which you were born, and its expectations. But meeting these expectations means nothing if it does not satisfy your inner self. Many people feel out of tune with their times and wish they lived in another age. This is quite normal for a large proportion of people born at any time. Some fit straight into the fashions and fancies of their generation while others just feel uncomfortable. This is why one needs to look beyond the year sign in astrology. The month and hour signs equally define a person.

The month sign represents the personality people display to their immediate families and friends. As with the year sign, some people are happier with their month sign than others. No one can escape the influences of their early family life, which colours their emotional responses for the rest of their lives. Our emotional wiring is laid down in childhood and anyone who thinks they can escape this is fantasizing. So, there are many people who will happily identify with their year and hour signs but draw back from their month sign. The first key to happiness is to accept who you are and that applies here. If you shrink from your month sign because its negative traits seem all too horribly familiar, the chances are that it is time to investigate the virtues of that sign and steer yourself towards them.

Your hour sign defines who you are on the inside, independent of family circumstances or the era in which you were born. Many people do not know their time of birth but in that case you may be able to guess by judging which of the animal signs you most relate to deep in your heart. Consider each in turn until one seems to fit, and unless you are totally lacking in self-awareness there is a good chance you will be right.

YIN AND YANG

HEAVEN AND EARTH UNITE IN THE IMAGE OF PEACE

THUS THE RULER DIVIDES AND COMPLETES THE COURSE OF HEAVEN AND EARTH

HE ADVANCES AND APPORTIONS THE GIFTS OF HEAVEN AND EARTH

AND SO AIDS HIS PEOPLE.

I Ching: the Image of hexagram 11, Tai (Peace)

The concept of Yin and Yang as the driving force of the universe is as basic to Chinese philosophy as that of the Five Elements. Even more basic, in fact, because all the accounts say that Yin and Yang were the first known forces. Combined in perfect harmony they formed the Cosmic Egg that was the only thing in existence. Everything else only became possible when this egg burst and the Yin and Yang were forcibly separated.

Their opposition is not, therefore, a hostile thing. Their interaction is the cause of the universe's fertility. Their differences are what make it tick along and produce such a glorious abundance and variety of life.

To Western ears, all this sounds quite acceptable and familiar until it is noticed that good and evil are not to be found in either category. Westerners traditionally relate black and white to evil and good and often leap automatically to the assumption that the Yin-Yang disc is just another expression of this duality. But this is wrong. Yin and Yang are equally good in Chinese eyes. Evil is something else entirely that seeps through the cracks when Yin and Yang are not in harmony.

In China people tend to be much less ready to leap into heated arguments. Impoliteness is a great social disgrace and if people do get into fights or feuds the Chinese are noticeably slower to assume their enemy must be evil just because they are the enemy. Up to a point anyway – one must beware of making broad generalizations. Chinese society is, however, notably more polite than many others; and this probably comes from not having an ingrained belief that all life is a struggle between good and evil. Fights and feuds erupt just as they do everywhere else, but markedly less often and against an ancient backdrop of cultural disapproval of such behaviour. Having the Yin-Yang disc at the heart of its philosophy, in Chinese belief all war and disruption is seen as a failure of wisdom, however necessary they may occasionally be.

In history this in-built tolerance is shown by the relations between the settled, agricultural Chinese and the warlike, horse-riding nomads of the north. The centuries have been punctuated by wars between them, but often in the intervals quite good relations developed and the ruling dynasties frequently intermarried to cement good relations. And when, as happened, the nomads conquered China, they were rapidly absorbed into the mainstream culture.

In religion, this tolerance is shown by the remarkably peaceful coexistence (relatively speaking) of the two main religions – Taoism and Buddhism. Their two parallel pantheons of deities and bodhisattvas exist side by side in heaven, often sharing its palaces and duties. So one often finds statues of the Eight Taoist Immortals in Buddhist temples and in many Taoist tales the Buddha and Jade Emperor consult each other over the best course of action heaven should take on major issues.

TABLE OF OPPOSITES

YIN	YANG
MOON	SUN
EARTH	HEAVEN
MATTER	SPIRIT
DARK	LIGHT
FEMALE	MALE
PASSIVE	ACTIVE
RECEPTIVE	CREATIVE
YIELDING	FIRM
DOWN	UP
WATER	FIRE
WINTER	SUMMER

THE KEYS TO HAPPINESS FOR THE SIGN OF THE GOAT

No matter what your sign, the first key to happiness for anyone is accepting who you are. The world is full of people trying to be something they're not and if it is glaringly obvious that you are a Goat by nature, it is no good wishing you were a Dragon instead and trying to behave like one. You will only make a mess of it. The true measure of success in life is written in our hearts; all the acclaim in the world is empty if it is for something you are not really proud of inside.

So if you do fit into the pattern of the Goat, the first thing to do is to accept and investigate the virtues and pitfalls of the sign, and the virtues are many. The Goat is a civilizing influence. It is the patron or practitioner of the arts which raised us out of savagery. Some people shine in times of war, others in times of peace and the Goat is chief among them. The Goat is the artist whose vision opens other people's eyes to the beauty around them. What they give to their communities is so subtle it often goes unnoticed until it is taken away and the group starts to fall apart without them.

Conflicts within your signs are not to be considered too ominous. They can cause real problems but only if you try to ignore or override them. Take what superficially appears to be the worst possible combination – a Goat year sign with an Ox month and a Dog ascendant (hour sign). The Ox and the Dog are the Goat's greatest natural enemies so you may think your chart is the recipe for a messy life; but the Dog and the Ox happen to get along very well with each other. What can result is a person who is confident and at peace within themselves, but feel they have been born at the wrong time. Such people can usually even tell you which era they would rather choose, when their tastes on all levels would have suited the fashions of the time. An interesting exercise is then to compare the time's year sign (if it can be narrowed that far) with the person's month and hour signs and see how they correspond.

The Goat is a lucky sign in many ways, not least because it gets along easily with most of the others. Goats are generally popular because by temperament they are friendly, accommodating, generous and don't get into arguments or rivalries just for the sake of it. They tend to attract comfortable wealth without too much effort. Just as a Year of the Dragon tends to have an exciting flavour for everyone, so a Year of the Goat tends to have an overall mood of calm and recuperation for all signs. Some like this more than others, of course. The Ox gets a bit impatient with the holiday mood and the Tiger, the Dragon and the Horse get restless for adventure towards the end, but overall it is a lucky year and money tends to flow a bit easier than usual for everyone.

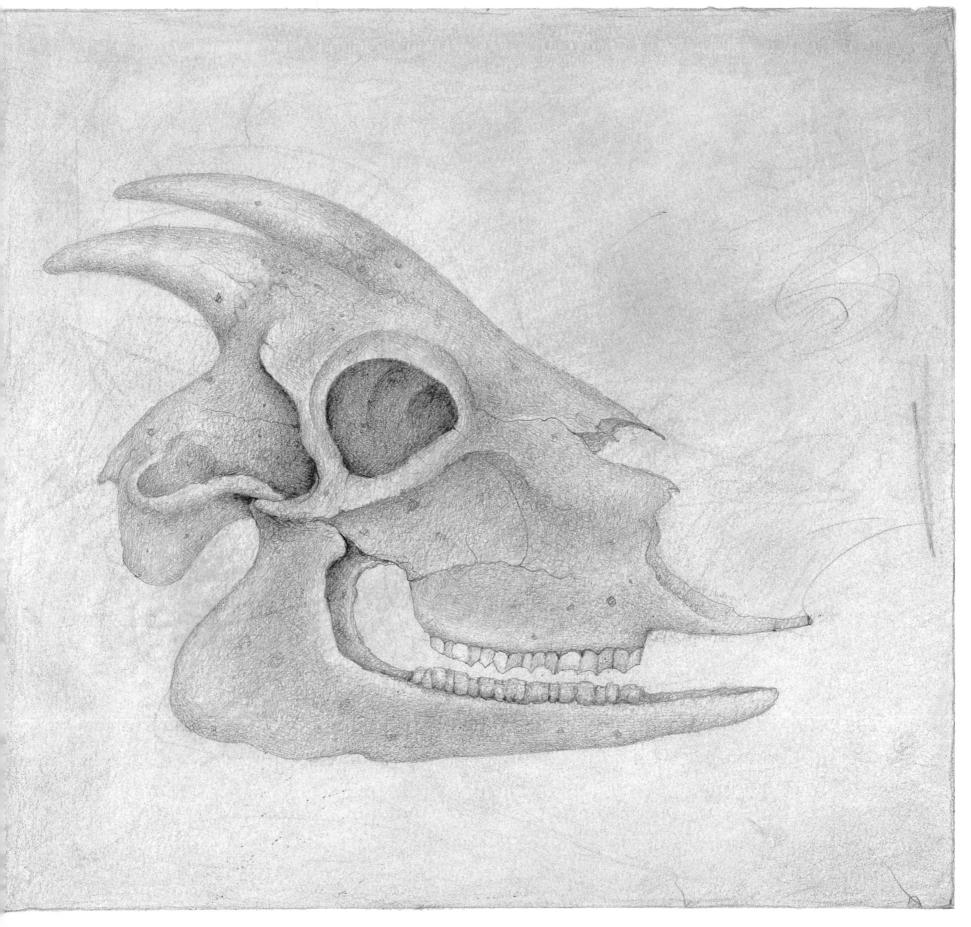

THE FUTURE FOR THE SIGN OF THE GOAT

2003

WATER GOAT

Being in its own sign means this should feel a good year for the Goat. Work and family pressures should ease, allowing time for private interests. You've probably earned a rest after the possibly alarming excitements of last year, so make the most of it. But don't relax too much and fall into pure self-indulgence. You still have responsibilities and challenges to face. This is a good year for defining who you are to friends and family. Be more assertive than usual.

2004

WOOD MONKEY

The Monkey, being a great trickster, will have a few surprises for you this year, but they will mostly be pleasant ones. Keep your eyes open and expect the unexpected. Your diplomatic skills are likely to be in demand for family disputes and you will need to be more careful than ever not to take sides. Apart from that, you should find this a good year in which to get ahead. Because you are so busy you may find yourself getting along with Ox people better than usual, but don't expect this to last.

2005

WOOD ROOSTER

Not a particularly good year for finances so, being a bit lax in that regard anyway, the Goat will have to be extra prudent. Resist the temptation to splash out on non-essentials, but otherwise it should be an interesting year with more social events than usual. Last year's family problems will continue and maybe come to a head, particularly if there are teenagers involved, but there should be nothing to cope with that is beyond your skill.

2006

FIRE DOG

An uncomfortable year for the Goat but the exercise of patience and good humour will reap benefits in the future. Bear this in mind when all your best efforts pass unnoticed and there seems no end to the demands on your time and energy. Tough years like this are needed from time to time to put iron in the soul and make us appreciate easier times, such as next year.

2007

FIRE BOAR

Here comes the sign of the Goat's great friend and last year will soon seem like a bad dream. Suddenly, you will find yourself being appreciated and surrounded by friends who cannot do enough to help you. Relax and have a well-earned rest. Relax those purse-strings too, because you are allowed to indulge yourself a bit. Your finances should get an unexpected boost or two this year, so throw a party to celebrate and share your good fortune. This is a good time to catch up with old friends and make a few new ones.

2008

EARTH RAT

This should be a good career year for the Goat, time to put into practise those ideas you've been toying with and take the lead for once. You'll find that all the support you've given others in the past now gets its reward because people will be happy to listen and to try out your suggestions. Don't step too much out of character by getting involved in work politics, though. Being a peacemaker is still your essential role and your colleagues rely on you for that.

2009

EARTH OX

Brace yourself for an awkward time. The Ox is the Goat's natural enemy, so Ox years are rarely comfortable, especially when the element is Earth. However, as long as you are braced for it, things need not be too bad. Exercise patience and modesty, and beware of being over-sensitive to criticism, because plenty of it will come your way. A sense of humour is your best defence when the going gets tough, that and the knowledge that, as with everything, the conditions will pass.

2010

METAL TIGER

Now you can relax and lower your guard a bit since your Ox taskmaster has ambled off into the west and here comes the dashing Tiger to tempt you to play again. As ever, don't get too carried away. The sudden easing of demands and complaints can go to your head. Start imagining there is no need for caution at all and you'll be in for a nasty surprise. Some tricky challenges will present themselves, but nothing you cannot handle as long as you keep your head.

2011

METAL HARE

Here you are in the year of your best friend the Hare, so just relax and enjoy yourself. It is a good year for reassessing your life and clearing the metaphorical attic. Examine your daily routine for time-wasting habits that have long outlived their usefulness. This is a good time for Goats to make a virtue of their tendency to laziness by freeing up more time in their lives. Finances will not be particularly healthy this year, but neither should they cause any serious problems.

2012

WATER DRAGON

An exciting year for the Goat, along with everyone else; and the downside of it is real danger at times, but the Goat who is prepared for this should cope well enough. Your cautious instincts should serve you well and keep you from getting too carried away by other people's persuasive rhetoric, particularly if they are Dragons. Don't commit yourself to any schemes you don't fully understand and put a lock on your purse. You'll need that money for very practical expenses.

2013

WATER SNAKE

This should be a good year for the Goat with less drama than the last and real gains in your career without undue effort. Having a subtle mind itself, the Goat is quite at home with the Snake's way of doing things and so really begins to shine in colleagues' eyes. You will often find your advice being asked on a whole range of unrelated topics, but don't let this go too much to your head because you will not always be right. This is a good year for starting a new business.

2014

WOOD HORSE

You may feel threatened this year by political events beyond your control, so it might be a good idea to check your fallback plans are all up to date and fully functional. But the chances are that none of the dangers will materialize or affect you directly. In fact, this should turn out a very creative and satisfying twelve months when you come to look back on them, even if you can't fully appreciate it at the time. You will enjoy the closeness of your family though, and should let them know this.

2015

WOOD GOAT

Here you are back in your own sign. Having Wood as its element gives a harder edge to the sign than the last time it appeared, so expect to find yourself being more assertive than usual, bossy even. If you have any unresolved conflicts on your hands, this is possibly a good time to tackle them though you may shock people with uncharacteristic bluntness and force. It's a good year for new romances or maybe rekindling the fires of an old one. Indulge your partners and show them how much you care.

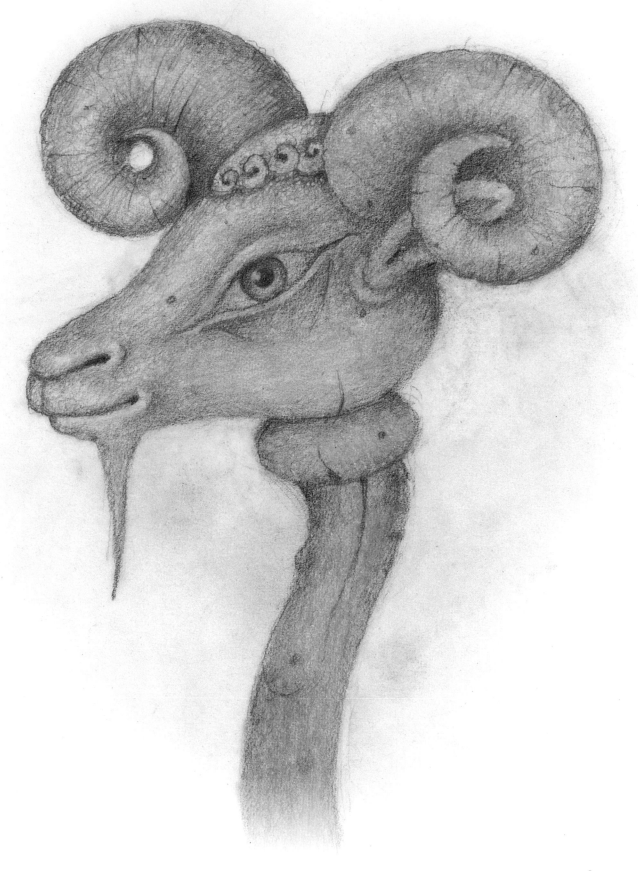

CONCLUSION

Chinese mythology is wonderful to outsiders for its combination of the strange and the familiar. The gods of China may be totally alien to outsiders but they act in many of the same ways as the gods of other cosmologies. The astrology has a similar appeal and also has the advantage of being infinitely easier for a newcomer to grasp than Western astrology. On the most superficial level of simply identifying with our birth signs, as defined by either system, they are equivalent. Each has twelve symbols that encapsulate certain aspects of behaviour that many people can easily identify with. But when you try and look a bit deeper in Western astrology you immediately run into quite tricky mathematical calculations involving latitudes and longitudes, planets and houses, whose meaning is far from obvious even after you have worked them out.

In Chinese astrology, all you need is your date and time of birth and an imaginative grasp of the twelve symbols. These simple requirements can give you a good picture of what Chinese astrology has to say about your temperament and likely fortunes. Instead of having to rely on the trustworthiness and insight of some claimed expert, you can judge its accuracy for yourselves. Do you feel that your year sign captures the mood of people your age? Do you recognise your everyday demeanour in the description of your month sign? Most of all, do you inwardly relate to the sign of your birth hour? These are questions anyone can answer without having first to spend a considerable amount of time studying the mechanisms of the system.

It can be taken a lot further than we have done here. Manuals the size of telephone directories are published annually in Chinese wherein you can also find your day sign and read what each day of a year is likely to have in store for you. The compilation of these requires massive calculations, but a very good grasp of Chinese astrology is possible without going anywhere near them. Armed with the information we have given here you should be able to get a very fair picture of what Chinese astrology has to say about people born under the sign of the Goat, and if that is your birth sign you should also be able to judge how apt it is. The curious thing about astrology is that while the modern rational mind can see no reason at all why the moment of birth should decide a person's character and fortune, astrology is often able to come up with insights that it is very hard to deny are true.

On top of all this, astrology is also a great way to become familiar with Chinese myth, legend and philosophy – beliefs underpinning the oldest civilization on the planet. Given the constancy of human nature around the globe, these can offer very useful insights into how anyone can conduct their life in order to make it a thing of beauty and harmony.

Also published by Pavilion:

YEAR OF THE DRAGON

2000 was the Year of the Dragon in Chinese astrology. This book offers a unique foray into the beliefs, and in a sense the reality, of dragons in China from only a few centuries ago. This charming travelogue leads the reader through the dragon-laden landscape of Chinese folktales and dragon lore from far-flung corners of the Chinese Empire.

YEAR OF THE HORSE

The Year of the Horse, 2002, investigates the sign of the Horse in Chinese myth, culture and astrology and exactly what it means to be born under this sign. The book celebrates the horse in all its guises, from the thundering war steed of the ancient Chinese warriors, to the gentle and mystical Qi-Lin whose appearance foretells the birth of a great Emperor.